Wind, Sand, and Sky

Wind, Sand, and Sky

by Rebecca Caudill

illustrated by Donald Carrick

E. P. Dutton & Co., Inc.   New York

Library of Congress Cataloging in Publication Data

Caudill, Rebecca   Wind, sand, and sky

SUMMARY: A poetic description of a desert and
its inhabitants.

1. Deserts—Juvenile poetry.   [1. Deserts—Poetry]
I. Carrick, Donald.   II. Title.
PZ8.3.C313Wi   811'.5'4   75-34113
ISBN 0-525-42899-2

Published simultaneously in Canada by Clarke,
Irwin & Company Limited, Toronto and Vancouver

Designed by Riki Levinson
Printed in the U.S.A.   First Edition
10 9 8 7 6 5 4 3 2 1

For Emily—
in love with all creation

The grizzled desert
  Holds fast its secrets and broods
    In the sizzling sun.

Lacy clouds drift by;
  On the far rugged mountains
  Lacy shadows lie.

The enormous sky
  Floats in space filled with the hum
  Of sweet, winey winds.

Gifts of the desert—
  Room enough, time enough, and
  Calmness after pain.

The brawny mountains
Throw their black shadows on fields
Of fragile poppies.

This year the sweet rains
    Spring-clean the earth and lay
       A flower-gemmed carpet.

Not so excited!
    There will be another spring,
       And yet another.

Morning dawns awry—
    A finch in a mesquite tree
       Sings to me all day.

Remember when we
   Lay in the sun envying
      Two eagles aloft?

Silence above me,
   Silence before, behind me,
      Silence within me.

Cones of golden sand
   Swirl across the desert floor—
      "Beat you to the gate!"

The summer storm comes
Bolting white lightning; it goes
Muttering thunder.

The tumbleweed, freed,
    Goes whirling across the desert
    In mad abandon.

Atop the saguaro
  Sits the hawk in his watchtower—
    Look sharp: mice, skunks, snakes!

Armed with barb, thorn, fang,
  And talon, the desert waits
    With prick and poison.

Decked in finery,
  Plumed, preened, no feather askew,
    Struts the knightly quail.

Autumn cottonwoods
Blaze like great yellow bonfires
Near the arroyo.

Rusty like the sand,
    A melody in motion,
        Lopes the coyote.

In the arroyo
    Where we found the tiny mice
        The white-gold grass stirs.

Azure, orange, green, red—
Clouds draw curtains of splendor
At the end of day.

Sunset. I loiter
Beside bird-laden mesquites
To hear the gossip.

Night comes on quickly,
    Snuffing out the dark mountains
    And lighting the stars.

I walk in starlight
And feel the throbbing heartbeat
Of the universe.

Soft in the darkness
They light the way of the Child—
Luminaria.

REBECCA CAUDILL holds a very special place in children's literature for her contribution of such stories as *A Certain Small Shepherd*, *Did You Carry the Flag Today, Charley?* (both Holt) and, most recently, *Somebody Go and Bang a Drum*. She has been honored many times, including the naming of the Rebecca Caudill Library in Cumberland, Kentucky. Her first book of haiku was *Come Along!*, illustrated by Ellen Raskin (Holt). She and her husband, James Ayars, live in Illinois but spend winters in Tucson, Arizona.

DONALD CARRICK's accomplished pictures have enhanced many fine children's books, including *Lost in the Storm* by his wife, Carol (Seabury), and *Bear Mouse* by Berniece Freschet (Scribner). For *Wind, Sand, and Sky* he visited the Ayars in Arizona. He took many walks in the desert, photographing, sketching, and finally just lying still on his stomach to observe the microcosmic life. He was able to research every detail, including the lighting of a luminaria.

The title display type is set in Weiss Italic enlarged, the other display type in Weiss Roman foundry, and the text in Weiss Roman linotype. The three-color art was prepared in watercolor. The book was printed by offset at A. Hoen & Co.